Introduction to
Photography

HOW TO PHOTOGRAPH
ABSOLUTELY EVERYTHING

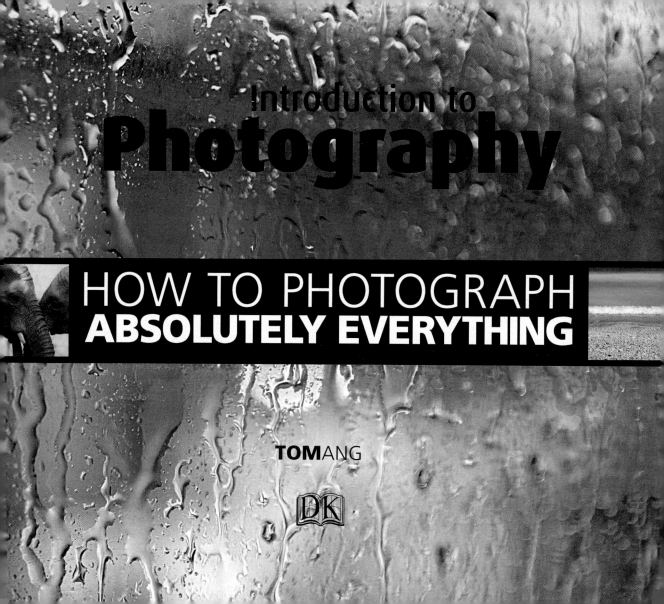

Introduction to
Photography

HOW TO PHOTOGRAPH
ABSOLUTELY EVERYTHING

TOMANG

DK

 LONDON, NEW YORK, MUNICH, MELBOURNE, DELHI

for Wendy

Project Editor Nicky Munro
Project Art Editor Jenisa Patel
Designer Sarah-Anne Arnold
Production Editor Vânia Cunha
Production Controller Melanie Dowland
Managing Editor Stephanie Farrow
Managing Art Editor Lee Griffiths
Cover Designers David McDonald, Nicoline Thilert

Produced on behalf of Dorling Kindersley by
Sands Publishing Solutions
4 Jenner Way, Eccles,
Aylesford, Kent ME20 7SQ

This Paperback edition published 2008
The material in this book originally appeard in
the book *How to Photograph Absolutely
Everything* first published in Great Britain in
2007 by Dorling Kindersley Limited
80 Strand, London WC2R 0RL

A Penguin Company

2 4 6 8 10 9 7 5 3 1

Copyright © 2007
Dorling Kindersley Limited
Text copyright © 2007 Tom Ang

ISBN: 978 1 4053 3768 7

Printed in Italy by
Rotolito Lombarda SpA
Reproduced by MDP in the UK
See our complete catalogue at
www.dk.com

1

Introduction to photography

6   Introduction
8   Elements of photography
12   Which digital camera do
     I choose?
14   What else to consider?
16   Camera settings
18   Finding focus
20   Judging exposure
22   Zoom settings
24   Framing images
28   Picture space
30   Time tips
32   Capturing light

34   Using colour
38   Brightness and levels
40   Colour balance and saturation
42   Contrast and tone
44   Removing distractions and
     sharpening
46   Cropping and resizing
48   *Acknowledgments*
     & Picture Credits

Introduction

This is a unique book, with a unique aim and daring ambition. I want to help you to know how to photograph any subject or situation you may encounter. Of course, it is essential to learn the basic techniques of photography. But that is like learning basic cooking techniques such as chopping, stir-frying, boiling. You have nothing edible until you add the ingredients. And to make a tasty meal you have to follow a recipe which works with and responds to the character of the ingredients to make the best use of them. This is a photographic recipe book. It shows how to create pictures by working with the basic ingredients of colour, light, and space – then "cooking" them up using techniques such as exposure, framing, and focus. By following the step-by-step recipes, you will steadily gain the ability to photograph absolutely everything. At the same time, the book brings together numerous tricks and tips that you may apply to a vast range of photographic challenges, empowering you to make the most of every photographic opportunity.

Elements of Photography

Elements of photography describes the building blocks that make up all photographs. Whether snapped on the simplest camera, crafted in the finest professional model, or made with scientific instruments, all photographs are created with light. And to create any image you must control the quantity of light and bring it into focus, while composing and timing the shot with precision. Here you will learn how to combine focusing, exposure, zooming, and framing with the ingredients of space, time, light, and colour, discovering how to make your camera work for you. You will also see how software can enhance your images by refining their shape, exposure, colour balance, contrast, and sharpness.

Which digital camera do I choose?

Today's digital cameras are universally capable of producing excellent results and offer a wide range of controls designed to make photography easy and fun. Cameras for the beginner fall broadly in to the simple point-and-shoot cameras with 3–4 megapixels and basic controls. Next up are those offering greater resolution – 5–7 megapixels – with more advanced controls and faster operating speed. Some of these models concentrate on quality with a zoom lens of limited range, while others offer a greater zoom range with a reduction in other features. More costly cameras will offer even greater resolution as well as more flexible camera and image controls or better lenses.

CONTROL SWITCH for changing camera mode or zoom setting (varies with camera model).

LCD SCREEN is the main interface with the camera, controlling framing as well as display of menu options.

SHUTTER BUTTON initiates the exposure sequence; good cameras respond quickly to pressure on the button.

INTERFACE HATCH covers the sockets for connecting to a computer or TV screen.

NAVIGATION ROSETTE is used to move through the menu and make settings.

FUNCTION BUTTONS are used to select display modes and delete images (varies with camera model).

ZOOM LENS with versatile zoom range.

MID-RANGE COMPACT

Modern compact cameras offer zoom lenses with at least 3x range (the longest focal length is 3x longer than the shortest) with sensors carrying 6 or more megapixels. In addition, all offer auto-focus, have a built-in flash, removable memory, LCD viewfinder (some have see-through viewfinders too), and a choice of different auto-exposure modes.

ADVANTAGES

>> Compact and light-weight
>> Easy to use
>> Capable of high-quality images
>> Inexpensive to run

DISADVANTAGES

>> Battery life may be limited
>> Display may be difficult to read
>> Range of accessories limited
>> Zoom action may not be smooth

MODE DIAL controls the operational mode of the camera, exposure metering, set-up and review of images.

POWER SWITCH for turning camera on and off; good models turn on quickly.

FREQUENTLY ASKED QUESTIONS

Q WHAT KIND OF VIEWFINDER IS BEST FOR ME?

A Liquid crystal display (LCD) viewfinders that flip out are useful for awkward angles. The larger the screen, the easier it is to use. Cameras with optical (see-through) viewfinders provide a small view but one that is easy to use in bright light and does not rely on batteries.

Q WHAT EXACTLY ARE MEGAPIXELS?

A Pixels are the picture's elements – the more you have available, the greater the capacity to record detail. The image sensor is made up of individual picture elements, so an 8-megapixel sensor is covered with 8 million individual elements.

Q HOW MANY PIXELS DO I NEED?

A 3–5 megapixels are ample for web use and for average-sized prints, while 8 or more megapixels are sufficient for many professional uses. However, the number of pixels does not guarantee good image quality – much depends on the lens quality and image processing.

MODE DIAL sets scene modes and other functions.

ELECTRONIC VIEWFINDER is a small LCD screen under a magnifier.

ZOOM LENS is much larger and offers greater zoom range and quality.

ZOOM LENS with limited zoom range.

BEGINNER'S COMPACT

Modern entry-level compacts suitable for the beginner represent exceptional value for money. They combine very good image quality with real ease of use in extremely compact and stylishly designed bodies. Some models offer moisture-proof bodies, some are extremely thin, others are chunkier for the larger hand. The range is broad and you can select with confidence.

ADVANTAGES

» Inexpensive to purchase
» Inexpensive to run
» Very easy to use
» Very light-weight and compact

DISADVANTAGES

» Zoom range may be limited
» May not accept accessories
» May be slow in operation
» May limit you as you progress

PROSUMER

Cameras that bridge the consumer and professional ranges – the prosumer – are capable of professional quality images, and offer a good range of photographic controls. They sacrifice sturdy construction in order to keep weight low and reduce size. Prosumer cameras accept flash and lens accessories as well as featuring high-performance lenses.

ADVANTAGES

» High-quality images
» Wider zoom range
» Accepts accessory flash unit
» May be rapid in operation

DISADVANTAGES

» Bulkier and heavier than point-and-shoot compacts
» More costly to purchase
» More complicated to use

What else to consider?

As your photographic experience grows, you may want to extend the range of your photography. As your confidence in your skills grows, you may start to stretch the capabilities of your camera. This is when you will begin to think about adding accessories to your camera. Some, such as a tripod or data storage, can be applied to any camera. Others, such as an accessory flash or a larger zoom lens, will depend on the facilities of your camera.

USING AN EXTRA FLASH

If you want to take photographs at parties or other events that take place indoors or at night, you will need an accessory flash. Your camera must have a way to connect the flash – usually through a hot-shoe in the top. Flash units with heads you can swivel and point in different directions provide the most control of the quality of light.

INCREASING ZOOM RANGE

If your camera has a modest zoom range – between 3x and 5x – it will not be long before you wish for an extension of this range. Just as with digital SLRs, in many cameras, zoom range may be extended by screwing on lens adaptors: wide-angle adaptors increase the field of view; tele adaptors increase the telephoto end of the range.

WIDE ANGLE

STANDARD

TELEPHOTO

EXTENDED TELEPHOTO

USING A TRIPOD

There is no doubt that a tripod is the best way to ensure sharp, high-quality images. Tripods also reduce the strain when you are waiting for a photographic moment, whether it is a setting sun or an animal moving across a landscape. A ball-and-socket head (above right) is light and easy to use, but a 3-way head (far right) gives the most control. Purchase the sturdiest tripod you can comfortably carry.

STORING DATA

The more you photograph, the more you will want to store. Modern data storage is amazingly affordable. You can back-up images onto CDs or DVDs using inexpensive writers (above right) and disks. For more rapid access, store images on portable hard-disk drives (right).

MEMORY CARD OPTIONS

Digital cameras store images on removable memory cards. The cards supplied with cameras are usually adequate for only a handful of images, so you will need to buy your own. Get the largest capacity you can afford, but you do not have to purchase the fastest cards as these are designed for professional cameras. It's a good idea to keep a spare card – deleting images as you go in order to make space is a practice guaranteed to result in you losing important pictures.

Q HOW CAN I BACK UP IMAGES WHILE TRAVELLING?

A Use portable hard-disk drives with built-in card readers. Insert your memory card, press a button, and the drive copies the contents of the card. When the operation is over, you can erase the card's data and start again.

Q HOW DO I DOWNLOAD PHOTOS?

A One method is to install the camera's software on your computer, then you will be able to connect it via a cable to transfer data. Alternatively, connect a card reader to the computer: remove the card from your camera, insert it into the reader and copy the files to the computer.

Q WHAT IS THE BEST WAY TO ORGANIZE MY PICTURES?

A Create a 'Pictures' folder if you do not already have one. Then create another folder named according to the location and date. Copy your pictures to that folder. When you open a picture to alter it in any way, immediately "save as" under a different name so you always preserve the original image.

PRINTING

Modern printers produce superb quality images and are inexpensive, but printing materials are often costly. Some printers connect directly with cameras, others read the memory cards. Both methods eliminate the need for a computer.

» DYE SUBLIMATION PRINTERS produce small prints of excellent quality very quickly and easily.

» INK-JET PRINTERS (above right) can produce very large prints but require you to prepare the image. Also, colour control may be tricky.

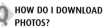

PRESENTING

There are numerous ways in which you can show your pictures to family, friends and, indeed, the whole world. Picture viewers (below left) store numerous images and display them on a screen.

» PICTURE-SHARING SITES allow you to upload images from any part of the world for storage and for others to view.

» PERSONAL WEBSITES can be constructed to show off your photographs in ways that you personally design and control.

Camera settings

Modern cameras emerge from their box with basic settings that will suit most photographers. But as you become more experienced and demanding in your photography, you will want your camera to do more. This means learning about its different settings and their effects.

USE YOUR CAMERA'S P FOR "PROGRAM" MODE. This gives you a high level of automation but allows you to make corrections or alter settings. The fully automatic mode – usually a green square or symbol – shuts off many adjustments, so is best avoided.

IF YOUR CAMERA OFFERS SCENE MODES – settings designed for situations such as landscapes, close-ups or sports – use them. They save a lot of button-pressing and scrolling through menus.

USE THE CAMERA'S HIGHEST QUALITY SETTING, but avoid the RAW or TIFF settings unless you have a specific need for these formats, such as printing large images. You can always reduce the size of the image but you cannot put back quality that is not already in the image.

IF YOUR CAMERA HAS ONE, USE THE BRACKETING SETTING to make sure you get the right exposure for your image. The camera will usually take three separate images at three slightly different exposures, and one of these should be correct.

CHANGE THE ISO OR SENSITIVITY SETTING OF YOUR CAMERA when working in dim lighting conditions. Raising the ISO number will make your camera more sensitive to light and enable you to use faster shutter speeds.

SET THE CAMERA TO SERIES EXPOSURE, RATHER THAN SINGLE EXPOSURE, if possible. This readies the camera to respond quickly if you need to make a number of exposures in rapid succession. If you don't need a series of images, you can just lift your finger off the shutter button.

USE THE AV (APERTURE VALUE) PRIORITY SETTING when the depth of field is an important aspect of your photograph. A high AV setting will capture a scene with a large depth of field; a low AV setting will produce an image with a narrow depth of field.

IF YOU HAVE TRAVELLED TO ANOTHER TIME-ZONE, remember to change the time setting on the camera. Accurate local time stamps on your images will help you to keep track of your pictures and store them in order when you return home.

SET THE CAMERA TO USE ADOBE RGB (if available on your camera) and set colour saturation (richness) and sharpness to increase by a notch or two in the camera's image adjustment menu to save work on your computer.

USE THE TV (TIME VALUE) PRIORITY SETTING when short or long exposures are necessary to suit the subject. You should use short shutter times such as 1/500 second for action, and longer times such as 1 second or more for blurred light trails at night. TV settings are represented as fractions of a second and can range from 1/8000 second to several seconds.

Finding focus

Virtually all modern cameras have auto-focus systems that almost guarantee the sharpness of some part of your image. But is the image sharp where you want it to be? The key to focusing is not just to focus the lens but to control where the sharpness lies. Most cameras will focus, by default, on the very centre of the image. While this is handy in most situations, it may lead to improperly focused images if the main subject of your image is not in the centre of the frame.

IF IN DOUBT, SHOOT ANYWAY. It is better to risk an unsharp image than having no image at all. If your image is a little bit on the soft side, you can always use your editing software to improve its sharpness.

DECIDE ON WHAT NEEDS TO BE SHARP AND FORGET THE REST. If you worry too much about technicalities like depth of field (how much of the scene appears sharp), your photography will be slowed down unnecessarily.

LEARN TO FOCUS ON ONE PART OF THE SUBJECT, hold down the button to keep focus, and re-compose for the shot. The more easily you can do this, the more your photography will improve.

IF YOUR CAMERA OFFERS A CHOICE BETWEEN MULTIPLE OR SINGLE FOCUSING POINTS, choose the single, central point. This allows you to focus more precisely and to focus past near obstructions such as railings or the leaves of a tree. In addition, the camera may work faster when set to a single focusing point, rather than several.

IF YOUR CAMERA IS UNABLE TO FOCUS, for example, because the subject lacks detail or is too high in contrast, point the focusing spot at another object that is the same distance away as your subject, before re-framing your shot and taking the picture.

IF POSSIBLE, SET YOUR CAMERA'S AUTO-FOCUS TO SERVO OR CONTINUOUS MODE when there is lots going on around you, or when your subject is moving irregularly and constantly changing its distance from you.

IF YOU SET THE AUTO-FOCUS TO SINGLE-SHOT or one-shot mode, the camera will expose only when it determines that focus has been found. This helps ensure sharp images but may slow down photography in fast-changing situations.

IF YOU HAVE MANUAL FOCUSING CONTROLS on your camera or lens, learn to use them. The controls on some point-and-shoot cameras may be very limited to setting focus by distance, rather than by watching the sharpness of the image. Manual control is useful when photographing close-up as it allows you to make precise adjustments in focus.

WHEN WORKING VERY CLOSE TO YOUR SUBJECT, it may be easier to keep it in focus by maintaining the distance between yourself and the subject by moving the camera backwards and forwards (nearer and further away) rather than by adjusting focus.

FOR SELF-TIMER SHOTS – where you set up the camera to include yourself in a group shot – ensure that the camera is not only framed correctly, but also focused on the group before you set off the self-timer. Alternatively, it may be easier to set the focus manually.

Judging exposure

Modern cameras and image manipulation techniques are close to making exposure problems a thing of the past. Many cameras actually analyze the scene and compare it with a database of known scenes to work out the best exposure. The result is that badly under-exposed images (too dark) or heavily over-exposed images (too light) are now much less common than before. But that is no consolation if one of your images has been incorrectly exposed. The key is to learn how to help the camera get the result you want.

IN TRICKY LIGHTING CONDITIONS, learn to obtain the exposure from the part of the scene you want exposed correctly, such as the face. Select the section of the image in the viewfinder, then hold the reading and re-compose the shot. This is the fastest way to ensure correct exposure.

IF IN DOUBT, MAKE THE EXPOSURE ANYWAY. It is better to have something that is not perfectly exposed than no image at all. You can always adjust the image later using editing software.

THE EASIEST LIGHTING SITUATION to expose for is when the subject is lit from the front, and the sun is behind you. However, such lighting does not give the most interesting textures.

WITH DIGITAL CAMERAS IT IS BETTER TO ERR ON THE SIDE OF UNDER-EXPOSURE. While even slight over-exposure tends to make colours look faded and washed-out, under-exposure can actually make colours (especially paler colours) look richer in tone.

TO REFINE YOUR EXPOSURE TECHNIQUE, use the centre-weighted or spot-metering mode to determine exposure. These read only a limited part of the scene, and you will learn by evaluating the results and making adjustments.

IN SUNNY SITUATIONS, try to position yourself so that the sun is to one side, so that you see your subject partially lit and partially in shadow. An exposure that takes in both the sunny and the shadowy areas is likely to be correct.

THE MOST DEMANDING LIGHTING CONDITIONS – against the light or high-contrast lighting, for example – make it difficult to obtain the correct exposure. If you have the opportunity, check the image and repeat the shot with extra or reduced exposure (using the override controls or manual exposure settings) as you need.

WHEN SHOOTING IN POOR LIGHT CONDITIONS, or if you or your subject is moving, you can reduce exposure times by adjusting your camera's sensitivity – the ISO setting. Raising it may enable you to take pin-sharp photos with little reduction in image quality.

EXPOSURE METERS WORK BEST MEASURING FROM MID-TONES – roughly half-way between lightest and darkest. Learn to recognize what mid-tones look like – lightly tanned Caucasian skin, green grass in half-shade, deep blue sky – and measure from that.

WHETHER AN IMAGE IS PROPERLY EXPOSED OR NOT depends on the type of image you want to create. You will have a key tone – a face, or flower, or patch of landscape, for example – that must look right, so expose for that. The rest of the image can fall in where it will.

Zoom settings

The combination of low price, top performance, and compact design in modern zoom lenses is one of the corner-stones of the success of modern photography. They put great optical powers into your hands, with the exciting prospect of being able to take command of all picture-making possibilities.

IF YOU HAVE A DIGITAL SLR, ADD MOVEMENT TO YOUR IMAGES by experimenting with the zoom effect. Set your camera to a slow shutter speed and, while the shutter is open, either zoom in to or out from the subject. For best effects, you will need to keep your camera as still as possible so that the motion lines are straight.

THE BEST WAY TO USE THE ZOOM is to decide what kind of picture or what part of the scene you want, then set the zoom to suit. Often you will want either the widest or the longest setting, but when you compose the image you can make small adjustments if you have time.

TRY SETTING THE ZOOM TO A FAVOURITE FOCAL LENGTH, for example, very long or very wide or half-way between, and leave it there for the day if your camera allows. You will find you can photograph more quickly and decisively when you are not always adjusting the zoom.

WHEN USING THE LONG END OF A ZOOM, be extra careful to hold the camera steady, since the chance of camera shake grows as focal length increases.

WALKING TOWARDS OR AWAY FROM THE SUBJECT IS OFTEN BETTER THAN ZOOMING IN OR OUT. It helps you to experience and explore changes in perspective, and keeps you actively looking for the best picture.

IF IN DOUBT, SHOOT AT A WIDER ANGLE and take in more of the scene. You can always crop an image afterwards, but you can't add to it once you leave.

AVOID USING THE DIGITAL ZOOM WHENEVER POSSIBLE. This is where the camera zooms as far as the lens will go, then increasingly small sections of the centre of image are enlarged for greater zoom. The results from digital zoom may disappoint, as the resolution is reduced.

IN DIM LIGHT, USE THE WIDEST ZOOM SETTING AVAILABLE as zoom lenses can gather more light (have a larger maximum aperture) at wide settings than at longer settings.

IF YOU WANT THE LINES IN AN IMAGE TO BE AS STRAIGHT AS POSSIBLE, for example, when photographing buildings, use the lens at around the middle of the range of zoom settings. Lenses tend to distort (bend) lines less at mid-range settings.

KEEP YOUR ZOOM LENS CLEAN. The lenses of modern compact cameras are very small, so the slightest smudge can have a significant effect on the quality of the image projected by the lens.

Framing images

Aiming the camera directly at a subject will ensure that it is "caught" in the picture. But exactly how you frame it is what can make the difference between a snap and a photograph. Framing is the process of choosing a camera position to create a composition that is visually effective. It is about ensuring that the elements in the picture, including colours and shapes, complement each other so that the picture communicates with the viewer in the way you envisaged.

MAKE SURE YOU HOLD YOUR CAMERA LEVEL – so that the horizon is level – unless you have a special framing effect in mind. In that case tilt the horizon strongly and obviously.

KEEP MOVING IN YOUR SEARCH FOR VIEWPOINTS, changing perspectives and variety in picture framing. If you are static, your pictures will also feel static and lacking in dynamism.

WHEN PHOTOGRAPHING SCENES WITH PEOPLE it is almost always better to be too close than to be too far away, so move in closer and keep up with the action.

TRY TO FILL THE FRAME right up to the corners. It is a good approach to keep visual interest going across the whole the image as far as possible, to give the viewer lots to look at.

PLACING THE MAIN SUBJECT OFF-CENTRE, closer to one side or the other, is usually (but not always) more effective than placing them in the dead centre. A useful starting point is to place your main subject roughly a third of the way into the image.

USE FRAMING DEVICES SUCH AS DOORWAYS, overhanging leaves, and out-of-focus features to form a natural frame to shape your picture. This helps to emphasize the subject, and give it context. It is also useful for hiding unwanted or distracting elements in the scene.

IF OBJECTS IN YOUR PICTURE ARE SIMILAR IN COLOUR OR DARKNESS, frame to keep them separate – with some of the background in between them. Otherwise, their shapes may become confused.

WHEN COMPOSING VISTAS OR SCENICS, try to place elements in the foreground; this gives a sense of scale and dynamic space. Allow the foreground interest to be out of focus to draw attention to the backgroound.

IF THE OBJECTS IN YOUR SCENE ARE EASY TO DISTINGUISH FROM EACH OTHER – for example, one is dark, another is light-coloured – you can try to overlap them, to give a sense of scale and receding distance.

WHEN SHOOTING LANDSCAPES, try pointing the camera high so there is only a narrow strip of land in the bottom of the picture – this helps give a sense of open space. Don't be afraid of exaggerating the difference in proportions in your picture.

Picture space

Photographs are records of scenes that occupy three-dimensional space. As a photograph – whether it is on paper or on a screen – stretches only over two-dimensions, photographers must somehow capture a sense of depth and space for the viewer. The tricks of composition help you to convey a sense of space in your pictures, while choosing your viewpoint carefully can help the viewer to interact with your picture.

THE EASIEST WAY TO SHOW THAT ONE OBJECT IS CLOSER THAN ANOTHER is to capture it overlapping and partially covering the furthest object. Control of overlap is a powerful way to convey space and describe spatial relationships.

"NEGATIVE SPACE" is a photographic term for empty space that contains no subject matter. You can use common examples of negative space, such as sky or water, to help define or give a backdrop to the main subject of your photographs.

ANOTHER WAY TO SHOW DIFFERENCES IN DISTANCE – and hence the space between subjects – is through differences in focus. Focusing on the main subject in the midground, and throwing the background and foreground out of focus, helps locate the subject.

ENCLOSE YOUR MAIN SUBJECT IN A FRAME such as an archway, window, or branches of a tree. In this way you will guide the viewer's eyes towards the main subject. Because your subject is shown to be further away than the frame, this will give an impression of travelling through the picture.

LINES CURVING THROUGH THE IMAGE SPACE lead the viewer's eye on a journey through the picture. This helps give a lively sense of composition, and keeps the viewer's attention.

YOU CAN REDUCE THE SENSE OF SPACE between elements in your picture by using the longest focal length setting. This gives a magnified view of a distant part of the scene, which compresses space, making objects appear to be almost touching when, in fact, they are far apart.

USE RECEDING LINES such as railings, a road, a wall, or a railway line to lead the eye from the foreground to the background. The convergence of parallel lines gives very strong clues about depth in the picture.

WHEN TAKING LANDSCAPE PHOTOGRAPHS YOU CAN EVOKE WIDE-OPEN SPACES and the majesty of the landscape by filling most of the frame with an open sky.

WHEN PHOTOGRAPHING A DISTANT OBJECT, such as a building or structure, one effective trick is to find something very close to you and position yourself so that the nearby object is in frame and out of focus, with the main subject in focus. Creating foreground interest in this way helps exaggerate the sense of space and distance.

FOR SOME SUBJECTS, SUCH AS BUILDINGS OR MONUMENTS, IT CAN BE USEFUL TO ALLOW SPACE ON ALL SIDES OF THE PHOTOGRAPH to frame your image. Too tight a crop on the subject's outline can make it feel trapped and have an unpleasing effect on the eye. By giving your subject space to breathe you can also add context to your image.

Time tips

Photographers are masters of time: we use and control time at two levels. There is the broader, larger time-scale of days, weeks, and months that determines the seasons of our photography. The low light either side of winter offers soft effects and long shadows, but short days. In contrast the long days of high summer sun give us hard light and high contrasts. Then there is the small-scale time – the fractions of a second that determine whether our images are sharp, or catch the smile or peak of action. Some photographs depend on waiting long hours or even months for the right lighting, but the precise timing is not so vital. Other photographs depend entirely on split-second timing for their success.

THE BEST TIME TO TAKE PHOTOGRAPHS IS WHEN YOU FIRST SEE THE OPPORTUNITY. Many modern digital cameras are so small and light that you can carry them with you everywhere. You can be ready to take photographs at any time, without delay, without having to promise yourself that you will return the next day with your camera.

WHEN YOU TAKE ANY PHOTOGRAPH YOU ARE FREEZING A MOMENT IN TIME, but this is particularly evident in action shots. To capture sharp images of moving subjects your exposure should be as short as possible – no longer than 1/250 second, but preferably 1/500 second for subjects like action sports or moving animals.

THE BEST TIMES OF DAY FOR TAKING PHOTOGRAPHS OUTSIDE ARE THE "GOLDEN" HOURS just after sunrise and just before sunset. At these times the sunlight is softened by the atmosphere, giving it a warm hue that makes landscapes and buildings glow.

TRY SHOOTING MOVING WATER AT SLOW SHUTTER TIMES. You will find that scenes of waterfalls, mountain streams, or lapping tides are transformed from being frozen and static to being alive and evocative.

EACH TIME AND SEASON OFFERS ITS OWN KIND OF LIGHT. Work with whatever light is offered to you: whether it is hard or soft, coloured or neutral, plentiful or scarce, all light is wonderful.

USE THE "BULB" SETTING ON YOUR CAMERA TO ACHIEVE VERY LONG EXPOSURE TIMES. These are particularly effective when taking photographs at night, when over a period of a few minutes you can capture star trails as they move across the sky, forked lightning during storms, or fireworks as they explode one after another.

YOUR CAMERA MAY BE SLOW TO RESPOND to being turned on or to the press of the shutter button. You may need to account for any delays by leaving the camera on stand-by rather than turning it off, or by releasing the shutter a little before you want the exposure.

WHEN TRYING TO CAPTURE A MOMENT OR EVENT, your sense of timing is vital. Try to anticipate the action by watching and learning repeated or regular patterns of behaviour or occurrances.

WHEN TAKING PHOTOGRAPHS OF A MOVING SUBJECT, you can capture the sense of movement by choosing a longer shutter time. As the subject moves through the frame its image will blur in the direction of its path. Alternatively, using the same shutter setting, you can pan along with your subject, so that it remains sharp but the background is blurred.

Capturing light

For some people, photography is primarily about capturing light itself, and the subject comes second. In some instances light can turn even the most mundane scene into a visually captivating image. While you may not be able to control the weather, nor position the sun to order, you can wait for the light, or position yourself to make the best of it. Lighting is intimately linked to camera exposure: correct exposure brings out the best in dull lighting but inaccurate exposure can ruin great lighting.

SHAFTS OF LIGHT, such as those cast through a forest canopy, create natural spotlights that you can use to capture subjects with dramatic effect.

HIGH-CONTRAST LIGHTING – where the difference between light and dark areas is great – can give you striking results, but is tricky to expose for. Shoot lots of frames at different exposure settings to learn which give the best results.

USE STRONG SHADOWS produced by harsh sunlight to create interesting patterns or to balance your compositions. You can also use shadows to create an impression of depth or space, and to lead the eye.

FOR THE MOST INTERESTING LIGHTING, try facing the light and place your subject in between. In these contre-jour ("against the day") situations you can obtain dramatic silhouettes, place the sun in shot for flare effects, and experiment with dramatic, dark skies.

WHEN SHOOTING PORTRAITS, it is very little trouble to ask the subject to move close to a window or out of the direct sun. Soft but directional light gives the most satisfying results in portraiture.

IN VERY BRIGHT CONDITIONS, USE THE FLASH TO REDUCE SHADOWS.
Set the fill-in flash or synchro-sun mode (modern point-and-shoot cameras do this automatically) and turn the flash on. This can help reveal details and colours that would have been otherwise hidden.

USE YOUR HAND TO CAST A SHADOW OVER YOUR LENS.
This reduces the effect of the sun shining into the lens, which causes flare – distracting reflections in the image. This may be necessary as many point-and-shoot cameras do not have effective lens hoods. But make sure your hand does not intrude into wide-angle shots.

WHEN THE LIGHTING IS TRICKY, and it is important that you have the correct exposure, try different settings to make sure you get the shot. You can take a look at the images after each exposure and delete those that you are not completely happy with.

WHEN TAKING CLOSE-UP PHOTOGRAPHS in full sunlight, use a piece of paper to diffuse and soften the light. This helps to deliver rich colours and delicate textures.

PHOTOGRAPHS CAN BE TAKEN IN THE DULLEST LIGHT. Even if the scene looks unpromising and too dark, have a go. The results may surprise and delight you because the camera can see more colours at night than you can.

Using colour

One of the steps to being able to photograph anything is being able to separate your experience of colour from the recording of colour in a photograph. This will help you to appreciate that the way in which a camera senses and records colours differs from the way that we see them – a captured image is never quite the same as we perceive it. But, more importantly, your versatility as a photographer improves the more you see colour as a subject in itself, not something that is only a feature of your subject.

COLOUR CAN BE ONE OF THE STRONGEST COMPOSITIONAL TOOLS IN PHOTOGRAPHY. Try isolating a strong colour against a muted background to emphasize the shape of an object or the perspective in a scene. You might also try picking out a small area of colour within a sea of contrasting colours and use it as a focal point.

COMPOSE YOUR IMAGE SO THAT THE RANGE OF COLOURS IS LIMITED to similar hues – different shades of green, or a variety of warm colours, for example. The colours will compose your image and give it internal harmony.

IF YOU PHOTOGRAPH A SCENE CONTAINING A RIOT OF DIFFERENT COLOURS, try to organize it so that very strong lines of composition run through it, or try to group the colours together. Alternatively, capture colours against a dull background such as grey or black – this is particularly effective in city scenes.

COLOURS ARE USUALLY AT THEIR MOST VIVID or saturated in semi-diffused light, such as that on a partially cloudy day. This is because the diffused light prevents strong highlights or glossy surfaces from causing a reduction in colour richness.

SLIGHT UNDEREXPOSURE CAN IMPROVE COLOURS in photographs taken using a digital camera. This applies particularly to light, bold colours such as yellows and reds, which can otherwise appear washed out and faded.

ALTHOUGH YOU CAN CORRECT THE COLOUR BALANCE of your photographs using image manipulation software, try to use the white balance setting on your camera to avoid either yellow-orange or bluish hues.

YOU CAN STRENGTHEN COLOURS – that is, make them more saturated – using a camera setting. This setting may be called "Enhanced" colour. However, some cameras produce strong colours by default, so it is best to experiment with the settings to find the results you like most. If you can get it right "in camera" this will save you having to work on the images on a computer later.

COLOURS ARE KEY TO CONVEYING MOOD AND EMOTION. A limited, muted colour scheme, such as cool blues and greens, can give an overall feeling of peace and tranquility. Highly contrasting bright colours can give an instant impression of high-energy and excitement.

THE JUXTAPOSITION OF PRIMARY COLOURS can provide your images with great visual potency. Mix swatches of blue, red, and yellow to produce dramatic images that make a statement.

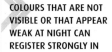 **COLOURS THAT ARE NOT VISIBLE OR THAT APPEAR WEAK AT NIGHT CAN REGISTER STRONGLY IN AN IMAGE.** This is because when our eyes are adapted to night vision they are not able to distinguish colours easily, but neither film nor digital cameras have problems with picking out different colours.

Brightness and Levels

Exposure controls the overall brightness of an image. Ideally you should not need to alter this using image manipulation software as the camera should have got it right in the first place. But the way you want the image to look often does not match what the camera has produced. So you need the Levels adjustment to make the broad changes in overall brightness. The Levels control also enables you to adjust the contrast – how quickly grey changes to white or to black.

IT IS ACCEPTABLE FOR SOME IMAGES TO LOOK VERY DARK OR NEAR BLACK. These include night shots, of course, but also shots that emphasize a focus of light on small areas of an image, such as a face, for example.

THE AUTO LEVELS COMMAND CAN OFTEN FIX AN IMAGE INSTANTLY, but manual levels adjustments will yield more controlled results.

LEVELS CAN CONTROL THE MID-TONE CONTRAST by changing the relationship between black and white. This either compresses white and black close together to give you high-contrast or spreads them out to give you more gentle tonal transitions.

HIGH CONTRAST

LOW CONTRAST

MANY CAMERAS CAN DISPLAY A HISTOGRAM when pictures are reviewed, and all image manipulation applications show a similar display in the Levels control. It represents what proportion of the picture is at different tonal ranges, which helps you work out what to do with the image. Here, to compensate for any over-exposure you would move the middle slider towards the peak of the histogram.

IF THE HISTOGRAM SHOWS MANY INDIVIDUAL NARROW BARS, like the teeth of a broken comb, the image is of poor quality. Further manipulation will not improve it, and it may print with colours markedly different from those on screen (neither your printer nor screen is faulty in this case).

IT IS ACCEPTABLE FOR SOME IMAGES TO LOOK VERY BRIGHT or near white. Pictures such as a bride in her white outfit, white pottery on a white background, or snow scenes, are naturally light and not necessarily over-exposed. However, for very bright images it is always a good idea to experiment with contrast and brightness, to see if you can improve the image.

AN UNDER-EXPOSED IMAGE LOOKS DARKER THAN AVERAGE. Shadows will show little detail and highlights may not be bright. Colours may look grey and dark, but colours in bright light may look deep and rich.

ORIGINAL IMAGE   ADJUSTED IMAGE

AN OVER-EXPOSED IMAGE LOOKS BRIGHTER THAN AVERAGE. Shadows will show a lot of detail but bright parts of the image will look bleached out, offering weak colours. Note that after adjustment, the white areas still look too bright.

ORIGINAL IMAGE   ADJUSTED IMAGE

ADJUST THE BLACKS SO THAT THEY LOOK BLACK. This ensures that you have nicely solid shadow densities when you print out the image. Lack of good blacks makes a print look washed-out.

ORIGINAL IMAGE   ADJUSTED IMAGE

Colour balance and saturation

Balancing colours is important as it helps ensure that the colours in your image are true to life. The key is to ensure that colours which everyone can recognize are accurate. Of these, the most important is skin colour: any visible variation from what is expected will make the whole image look wrong. The other key colours are the so-called "achromats": white, black, and grey. As the name suggests, these tones should be without colour or tint for colour reproduction to be accurate.

MODERN COMPUTER MONITORS ARE FAIRLY ACCURATE AT REPRODUCING COLOURS, but if you find that the prints from your printer are very different from the image as seen on your monitor you will need to use the monitor control panel or system preferences in your computer's operating system to calibrate the screen.

SKIN TONES, IF PRESENT, ARE THE KEY TO COLOUR BALANCE. If skin appears too cold or too warm you can be sure the rest of the image is unbalanced. Adjust the balance control in your software until skin appears natural.

ORIGINAL IMAGE ADJUSTED IMAGE

DECREASING SATURATION BRINGS COLOURS CLOSER TO SHADES OF GREY, BLACK, AND WHITE. Reducing colour saturation completely leaves you with a black-and-white or monochrome picture.

ORIGINAL IMAGE

ADJUSTED IMAGE

THE EASIEST WAY TO ADJUST COLOUR BALANCE IS TO USE THE VARIATIONS COMMAND. This shows, at a glance, the effect of different settings. All you have to do is click on the one that looks most natural or closest to the colours as you remember them.

COLOURS OR HUES CAN BE DELIBERATELY DISTORTED to give a strongly graphic effect. All colours are distorted by the same degree, so, for example, blues become greens and reds turn mauve.

ORIGINAL IMAGE

ADJUSTED IMAGE

TRY TO SET THE CAMERA UP SO THAT YOU HAVE TO DO AS LITTLE COLOUR ADJUSTMENT AS POSSIBLE AFTER MAKING THE EXPOSURE. Many digital cameras allow you to adjust colour richness, as well as the contrast and sharpness that is applied to the image when it is saved on the memory card. Use these features to optimise your pictures for viewing or printing to save time and effort.

COLOURS LOOK MORE LIVELY AND PUNCHY when you increase their saturation. However, colours that are too highly saturated may look brilliant on a monitor screen but cannot be printed accurately. Prints on paper may appear pale because some printers cannot reproduce the brightest colours.

ORIGINAL IMAGE   OVERSATURATED

YOU CAN REMOVE COLOUR FROM PICTURES BY USING THE SATURATION (OR SPONGE) TOOL TO DESATURATE – that is to reduce the strength of colour. This is effective at reducing the impact of a busy or colourful background that distracts from the main subject.

ORIGINAL IMAGE   ADJUSTED IMAGE

Contrast and tone

Contrast is the relationship between the middle greys and the whites and blacks – how the middle tones relate to the lightest and darkest tones in a picture. Contrast is largely the product of the lighting at the time you make the exposure, but it is also something that is easily altered on a computer, using image manipulation software. The careful adjustment of contrast and its suitability for the subject is a hallmark of fine photography.

HIGH-CONTRAST IMAGES SHOW AREAS OF DEEP SHADOWS and areas of bright white, with sharp transitions in-between. These images exhibit hard lighting, such as when directly lit by bright sun.

MOST PICTURE-EDITING SOFTWARE PROGRAMS have a contrast menu option with a slider for adjusting the contrast. However, you can alter the contrast and tone with more control by adjusting the Levels settings.

SOFTEN THE CONTRAST of images shot on brilliantly sunny days to bring back details into the brighter mid-tones and lighter shadows. This will make the printed image look more natural.

IMAGES WITH NORMAL CONTRAST show mostly middle-tones – greys about half-way between white and black – with some bright white tones plus some deep black, and with transitional tones in between.

LOW-CONTRAST IMAGES show large areas of middle or grey tones, with little that is either very dark or very bright – the look of a foggy day, for example. These images are said to be flat.

ORIGINAL IMAGE   ADJUSTED IMAGE

INCREASE THE CONTRAST IN BLACK-AND-WHITE IMAGES

to produce a stronger, more graphic picture. If the original is in colour, first convert it to black and white. Then increase the contrast until you achieve the desired effect. This technique works well with silhouettes with clear outlines, and with objects with geometrical shapes or strong patterns.

ORIGINAL IMAGE

BLACK-AND-WHITE IMAGE

ADJUSTED IMAGE

INCREASE THE CONTRAST IN IMAGES SHOT IN DULL OR OVERCAST CONDITIONS

to restore tonal depth and richness. You will find that, as well as making colours bolder and brighter, this will increase definition and bring out details in your subject.

ORIGINAL IMAGE   ADJUSTED IMAGE

IF YOU INCREASE THE BRIGHTNESS OF AN IMAGE,

you alter the relationship between greys, blacks, and whites, so a compensation in contrast may also be necessary. Look at each image on its own merits, and adjust the brightness and contrast until you are happy with the result.

ORIGINAL IMAGE   BRIGHTER IMAGE   ADJUSTED IMAGE

AN IMAGE THAT IS HIGH IN CONTRAST,

will appear to be sharper than one that is lower in contrast. This is because the margin between a white and a black area is seen as an edge, so the more marked the difference, the sharper the edge appears to be.

ORIGINAL IMAGE   ADJUSTED IMAGE

Removing distractions and sharpening

The best way to deal with distractions in your pictures is, of course, to avoid them in the first place. Care taken when you position yourself and point the camera to compose a picture will save you much effort later. But image manipulation software usually offers powerful tools for removing unwanted objects or unsightly elements. Once you have removed distractions, you may wish to sharpen the image, as this can help improve the appearance of your photograph, even if you have focused it correctly.

A STANDARD FEATURE IN MOST IMAGE MANIPULATION SOFTWARE IS A CLONE OR CLONE STAMP TOOL. This is one of the best ways of removing unwanted elements or distractions from your images. It works by copying or sampling one part of an image and pasting it onto another. For example, you can place a sample of sky onto tree branches or electricity pylons to make them disappear.

ORIGINAL IMAGE — ADJUSTED IMAGE

INSTEAD OF SPENDING TIME REMOVING DISTRACTIONS, try blurring them (using a blurring or smudge tool) in order to make them less sharply delineated and obvious. This is effective because the eye favours objects with sharp contours or edges. To blur a section of an image, first you will need to select it using one of the selection tools.

ORIGINAL IMAGE — ADJUSTED IMAGE

ANOTHER KIND OF DISTRACTION IS NOISE, which is a by-product of setting very high sensitivities (high ISO ratings such as 800 or greater). It gives a grainy look to the image. Many image manipulation software packages contain filters that can remove noise from an image, including dust and scratches.

ORIGINAL IMAGE — ADJUSTED IMAGE

IF YOUR IMAGE IS A LITTLE SOFT OR BLURRED, USE A SHARPEN FILTER TO INCREASE ITS SHARPNESS. You can sharpen the picture by as much or as little as you like by adjusting filter settings.

ORIGINAL IMAGE   ADJUSTED IMAGE

WHEN SHARPENING AN IMAGE FOR PRINTING, it should look slightly over-sharpened on the screen, so that artefacts such as exaggerated borders are only just visible at full size (viewing at 100 per cent). For on-screen use, for example, in websites, sharpen your images only until they look right on screen.

INCREASING THE CONTRAST OF AN IMAGE GIVES AN IMPRESSION OF INCREASED SHARPNESS. Ensure that the image is at the correct contrast before using a filter to increase sharpness.

ORIGINAL IMAGE   ADJUSTED IMAGE

IF YOUR CLONING PRODUCES AN UNNATURALLY SMOOTH-LOOKING AREA, you may need to introduce some noise to make it look more natural. Select the area to be worked on and apply the noise filter. Alternatively try changing the settings on the clone tool such as the hardness of the brush edge and also the opacity – how strongly the clone is applied to the image.

GENERALLY, SHARPENING SHOULD BE THE VERY LAST FILTER YOU APPLY – following other manipulations such as cropping, resizing, and adjusting levels – because of its very strong effects on image data. After applying the sharpening, check the image at 100 per cent magnification for any defects that the sharpening may have revealed.

USE SHARPENING FILTERS SPARINGLY. These filters sharpen pictures in a magical way, and reduce the effect of mild blur, but too much of a good thing can cause artefacts, such as contrasting haloes and exaggerated borders, to appear around your subject. It can also increase noise, making the image look as if it is composed of rounded grains of sand.

Cropping and resizing

One of the most basic things you do with a digital image, either before or after making any other adjustments, is ensure that it is the size you need it to be. Changing the size does not alter its appearance, but can make it easier to send by wireless or email, or to ensure that it comes out the right size for your printing paper. You will also need to crop the image a little if you need to straighten out horizons that are not quite level.

CROPPING REDUCES THE SIZE OF AN IMAGE, and throws away information, so severe crops should be reserved for large images. When you crop an image and then try to view it at the same size as it was before it was cropped you will notice that the pixels are larger.

ORIGINAL IMAGE

ADJUSTED IMAGE

THE FIRST THING TO DO WITH YOUR IMAGE BEFORE YOU WORK ON IT IS TO MAKE A COPY. Duplicating your image before you make any changes prevents you from accidentally saving any changes on to the original file and closing it, which loses the original forever.

CROPPING IS AN EFFECTIVE AND SIMPLE WAY TO ENLARGE PART OF AN IMAGE. In this way you can focus attention on the main subject if there is too much space around the edges.

ORIGINAL IMAGE

ADJUSTED IMAGE

YOU CAN CROP AN IMAGE TO REDUCE FILE SIZE, particularly if you are sure you do not need the elements you are removing. Even removing a narrow margin from a large image can offer a significant saving in file size.

CROPPING AND STRAIGHTENING CAN CORRECT TITLED HORIZONS. Draw a narrow crop near the horizon and rotate the crop so that it lines up with the horizon. Then extend the corners of the crop to the edge of the picture – two of the corners will meet the picture edge, but the opposite corners will be inside the picture. When you crop, the picture will be rotated correctly.

ORIGINAL IMAGE

ADJUSTED IMAGE

TO MAINTAIN THE ORIGINAL PICTURE'S SIZE RATIO, choose the crop tool, click and drag over the whole image (as if you want to crop the entire image), then hold down shift key and drag the crop box to the desired size. (This trick works for most image manipulation programs.)

CROP OUT DISTRACTING ELEMENTS or anything that doesn't add to the image, such as dominant colours, as the eye is drawn to bright objects first.

ORIGINAL IMAGE   ADJUSTED IMAGE

IF YOU CHANGE THE SHAPE OF YOUR IMAGE expect large borders – especially if you're having your pictures printed at an outlet – as these generally print only in standard shapes and sizes.

ADJUSTED IMAGE

ORIGINAL IMAGE

RESIZE THE IMAGE TO SUIT THE TASK. If you want to share images, either on the internet or by email, they seldom need to be more than 500 pixels wide, and at most 1280 pixels wide. This will give you very high quality for viewing on monitors. If you wish to make prints, you need to ensure that two settings are correct. Firstly, make sure that you have enough pixels for the size: a rule of thumb is to have around 300 pixels for every 1 inch of print. For example, a 12 x 10cm (5 x 4in) print needs an image measuring about 1500 x 1200 pixels – well within the capacity of all modern digital cameras. The other measure you need is the output size. This should be the size of print that you want, and it should fit the paper that you're using. Check this measurement in the image software.

Acknowledgments

AUTHOR'S ACKNOWLEDGMENTS

This book owes its production and creation, in crucial measure, to the Herculean efforts of project editor Nicky Munro; my warm thanks for her tireless contributions, which went a long way beyond the call of duty. Congratulations and thanks to Sands Publishing Solutions (Simon Murrell and David and Sylvia Tombesi-Walton), who turned a jumble of thousands of images and words into a clean, inspiring design.

I'm pleased to thank Andy Mitchell for the majority of photographs taken of me at work, but thanks also go to Wendy Gray, Nicky Munro, and Charlotte Crowther for the others.

I am also most grateful to those who modelled for me: Emma and John Owen; Joe, Annabel, and Bill Munro; Priscilla Nelson-Cole; Michelle Baxter; Su St Louis; James, John, Joe, and Ed Munro; Polly, David, Jack, Joe, and Billie Packer; Tracy, Peter, Hayley, and Ruby Miles; Wendy Gray, Wim Buying, Kyna Gourley, Jenisa Patel, Bronwen Parker-Rhodes, and Charlotte Crowther.

For their cooperation and access, many thanks to: Serafin Domenach of El Arca Animal Sanctuary, Guadalest, Spain; Yana Zarifi and her actors for access to *The Persians*; Jose Luis Quesada and Paula Albamonte at Ciudad de las Artes y las Ciencias, Valencia, Spain; Juan Llantada Sacramento of the Valencia Tourist Office and Jaime Samcho, counsellor of Valencia Cathedral for their help with the shoot at the cathedral; Steve Greenberg at 230 5th, New York; Jake at Pete's Candy Store, Brooklyn; Buffalino; Melinda Manning, assistant director for public relations at the New York Botanical Gardens.

For help during the New York shoot, special thanks to Su St Louis and staff of the Dorling Kindersley New York office, in particular Chrissy McIntyre and Michelle Baxter.

Many thanks to Kodak, Canon, Fujifilm, Panasonic, Nikon, and Ricoh for the loan of their cameras.

My special thanks to those who helped fill gaps in the photographic coverage, namely Chip Prager for his bird pictures; also to Wendy Gray, Andy Mitchell, David Summers, and Paul Self.

Above all, and as always, big thanks go to Wendy for her love and support, which make anything seem possible and enable much to be actual.

Tom Ang,
London

PUBLISHER'S ACKNOWLEDGMENTS

Dorling Kindersley would like to thank all those mentioned above and also: Tim Lane and Michael Duffy for design assistance; David Summers, Bob Bridle, Tarda Davison-Aitkins, and Simon Tuite for editorial assistance; John Noble for compiling the index.

Picture credits